Decision Making

John H. Van Vliet III, Ph.D. and Ramin L. Varnhorn

2017

Published by the
Institute for Leadership, Business and Public Policy
Young Harris College
1 College Street
Young Harris, Georgia 30582

ISBN-13:   978-0-9859373-1-7

Cover Photo: Ramin Varnhorn

Dedication

This book is respectfully dedicated to Zell Miller,
former Governor of Georgia, former Senator from
Georgia and Professor Emeritus at Young Harris
College. Governor Miller inspired Young Harris
College to combine the academic study of Business
with the academic study of Public Policy. He taught
Leadership to the YHC Classes of 2010 and 2011. He
continues to serve YHC as a shining role model and a
committed friend.

Table of Contents

The Authors

John H. Van Vliet III, Ph.D., US Army LTC (ret.) is the Professor of Business and Public Policy at Young Harris College. He has pursued three careers.

Military: He served 24 years as an Infantry officer including service with the 75th Ranger Regiment and duties with the Intelligence community

Business: He directed a large business unit in the distribution and automation engineering industry.

Education: His teaching began with Economics at West Point and spans instruction from middle school through graduate levels.

B.S., Engineering, United States Military Academy
M.A., Political Science, Georgetown University
M.B.A., Management, Georgia State University
Ph.D., Organization & Mgmt., Capella University

Dr. Van Vliet is married to his high school sweetheart. They live in Hiawassee, Ga., and have two grown daughters and three grandsons.

Ramin Varnhorn, a strong scholar, a fine soccer athlete, and a gracious gentleman, was recently graduated from Young Harris College with a Bachelor of Science in Business and Public Policy. He is presently pursuing internship opportunities in Europe where he intends to complete a Masters degree.

I. Introduction

People make decisions all the time. However, the experience of making everyday decisions is not sufficient to help managers make better decisions for their companies, organizations or agencies. The purpose of this book is to offer techniques that will help managers make better decisions.

Let's begin by getting a solid grip on what constitutes a "good decision" or a "better decision".

Good Decisions and Uncertainty

First, we should acknowledge that the decision making covered in this book takes place in the context of uncertainty. (Choosing between orange juice and apple juice for breakfast is making a choice between certainties. The outcome of selecting orange juice is certain, as is the outcome of selecting apple juice. Such a choice does not rise to the level of "decision making".) In a context of uncertainty, the decision maker knows the desired outcome, but is not sure what path will lead to the desired outcome.

It is tempting to suppose that a good decision generates a good outcome. That is not quite correct.

A good decision is one that has a better chance of reaching a good outcome than a poor decision has.

Here is an illustration of this concept:

The "Play or Don't Play" Decision

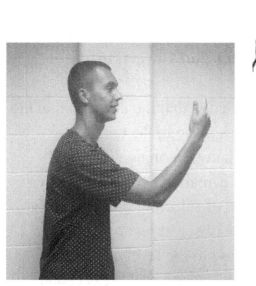

Suppose you are offered the chance to bet on an honest flip of the coin. If the coin lands "heads", you will win a dollar. If the coin lands "tails", you must pay a dime. Your option is to play or not play. Given that you have a 50% chance of winning a dollar balanced against a 50% chance of losing a dime, math tells you it would be wise to decide to play. Based on probabilities, it would be a "good decision" to decide to play. Now, suppose the coin lands "tails", and you lose your dime. Did you make a poor decision? No, you did not. The outcome was poor. Fortune or luck did not go your way. However, your decision put you in an advantageous position given what could be known before the coin was flipped. Accordingly, your decision was good, but the outcome was not.

There is a corollary here. Had you elected not to play, and the coin landed "tails", you might want to proudly note that you made a good decision because you avoided the loss of a dime. Actually, you made a lucky decision rather than a good one. Given the probabilities and the fact that the coin has not yet been flipped, the decision to play was the wise decision one should make.

Well, what about luck or chance? It would be grand if we could control luck, but we cannot. However, we can control the reasoning we bring to bear on probabilities in the face of uncertainty. Luck and chance are beyond our control. Reasoning is what we must depend upon.

The section above condenses into a simple concept:

> ➢ **A good decision is one that has a better chance of leading to a preferred outcome than to an undesired outcome.**

One can also note a corollary:

> ➢ **Good decisions do not always produce good outcomes.**

A subsequent concept arises:

> ➢ **It is wise to plan for bad outcomes.**

…..

All Decisions Are Not Equally Significant

This book covers some complex decision making techniques. Must every decision a manager confronts be subject to serious analysis? Obviously not! Some decisions are minor matters. A manager needs to handle such decisions swiftly and move on rather than spend valuable time and attention on matters of small consequence.

For instance, choosing to purchase a four-drawer filing cabinet or a two-drawer filing cabinet for a single office is a small matter. One would like the decision to be wise and well-made, but the cost of correcting a poor decision in this case is minimal. Make the choice and move on.

Other matters also require only a limited analysis. For example, a general manager of a distribution company had a customer bring him an odd minor problem that he resolved by taking direct action himself. That solution cost a good bit of "executive time", but it was easier (and less costly) for the manager to resolve the matter himself than to take the effort to show others what needed to be done. As the problem was "one off" (a problem that would probably not recur), it did not matter much that the solution was not efficient.

Some small matters do require careful analysis. Suppose the customer problem cited above was one that might crop up repeatedly. In such a case, even though the matter was minor, the sum of lots of minor incidents could become significant. In such a case, the manager would want to spend the time and analysis to find a solution that would effectively resolve the situation without burning too many resources. In addition, the manager might need to find a solution that is simple enough to be incorporated into "business as usual" for the organization. "Systemic" matters, even if they are minor by themselves, generally merit careful attention.

With that as a foundation, it is time to move on to consider what one can do to make better decisions.

II.   The Rational Decision Making Framework

The "Play or Don't Play" decision above was simple and clear. The outcomes were understood. The options were limited and known. The probabilities were defined. Obviously, real world decisions are made in contexts of much greater uncertainty. A deliberate structure can be valuable in such contexts.

Here is a good framework of the steps one might use in decision making:

Steps in Rational Decision Making
Define the Goal
Develop the Options
Evaluate the Options
Select the Best Option
Define Success or Failure
Implement the Decision
Review the Outcome

Let us consider each of the elements of the framework.

Define the Goal

One starts the formal decision making process by getting a solid grip on the desired outcome. (I have to emphasize this point as it is all too common for leaders and managers to lose sight of the goal as they become caught up in details and complexities of the options.)

Develop the Options

Given a clearly understood goal, the decision maker then needs to determine what options or choices are available.

Evaluate the Options

What are the potential outcomes and costs associated with the possible options?

Select the Best Option

Make the actual decision. Which option is best? (Please note there can be plenty of overlap between "Evaluate the options" and "Select the best option". After all, evaluation methods tend to classify some options as better than other options, so evaluating options tends to point towards a best option. Still, it is important to recognize the decision maker has the ultimate responsibility to choose, so we retain the formal step of "Select the best option".)

Define Success or Failure

This part is often overlooked, but it is important. How will you know if the selected option is actually generating a good outcome? (Remember, most situations are much more complicated than simply knowing if you won or lost the coin flip.) What tools will you use to measure success or failure? What measured values would cause you to declare success? What conditions would cause you to declare failure? Deliberately including this step in the decision making process will help you avoid the trap of committing valuable resources to an unwise attempt to rescue a poor outcome.

Implement the Decision

While technically not part of the decision making process, managers should recognize the importance of the steps needed to implement the selected option.

This is a classic management and leadership function as one communicates the plan, allocates the resources and supervises the actions. Clearly, picking the best option is only a start. One has to implement it well, or the outcome is less likely to be a good one. Thinking about implementing the selected option is also helpful as it might lead a decision maker to reconsider his choice. After all, it might be wiser to go with the "second best option" if the best option would be substantially trickier to implement.

Review the Outcome

The final step in the framework is a review of the outcome. What really happened? Did the organization achieve success or failure as defined in the earlier step in the framework? Such a review can lead to a new set of issues and choices and cause the organization to start a new decision making cycle.

. . . .

Let's look in detail at each part of the framework.

Define the goal

Defining the goal can be straight forward or quite troublesome. A good start is to try to write down the goal. If the goal can be described clearly in writing, then it is probably pretty well defined. For this to work, goals must be described in terms that are as objective as possible. Subjective goals often appear to be clear, but they are not.

For example, the subjective statement, "Our goal is to design a better process" sounds clear, but it is not. What does "better" mean? We can improve the goal by taking the effort to be more objective. For instance, we might change the goal to read: "Our goal is to alter our processes so we can serve at least 25 customers per hour without having to increase our staff."

The step of defining the goal is also highly important because of biases or pre-judgements that can creep into the process.

<u>Framing:</u> Defining the goal and framing the question are liked

Russo and Shoemaker (2002) emphasize the importance of properly defining (or "framing") the question or the issue under consideration. They note "frames are mental structures" people use to clarify, simplify and shape the complex and chaotic world around us. Shared frames help people understand one another and work together towards a common goal. Shared frames also have the effect of setting boundaries, sometimes unhelpful boundaries, to restrict our thoughts and actions. (To "think outside the box" is an expression praising the ability to overcome restrictive mental boundaries or frames.)

Here is an example of framing:

YHC Enterprises supplies drill bits to industrial clients who use the drill bits in machines that manufacture parts. One client insists on buying cheap drill bits that wear out quickly and need to be replaced. The sales rep for YHC enterprises wants to persuade the client's purchasing manager to buy more expensive drill bits which will last longer. The sales rep can show the more expensive bits last longer and actually make more "holes per dollar" than the cheaper drill bits. The sales rep will note the shared cost saving advantages of reducing the number of transactions and deliveries as well as the special cost savings to the client by having fewer shutdowns to replace worn out drill bits.

Suppose the purchasing manager (as is the typical case) is rewarded and praised for successfully negotiating lower prices. With this "frame" in place, the purchasing manager is not likely to see or value long term cost savings outside of his department. All the purchasing manager wants to see is a better price!

Now suppose the purchasing manager has a different and wider "frame", perhaps caused by a profit sharing motivation. In this situation, the purchasing manager would be interested in considering a solution that reduces costs for the company even if the price per drill bit goes up.

After we have defined the goal, it is wise to ask what sort of frames are in place in order to ensure you are comfortable with them. As a thought experiment, consider the example goal used earlier: "Our goal is to alter our processes so we can serve at least 25 customers per hour without having to increase our staff." What frames do you see?

With a well-defined goal in hand, we are ready for the next step.

Develop the Options

Ah… this part can be fun. It is also challenging because people tend to follow patterns, and many valuable options are only to be found outside the boundaries of typical or normal patterns. The best hope to generate a good set of options comes from including multiple people in the process of generating options and from deliberately seeking to be creative. Two specific processes can be helpful in this step. They are "brainstorming" and the "Six Thinking Hats".

Brainstorming is a technique that seeks to generate lots of ideas. It is understood many of the ideas will be impractical or even silly, but that is a small price to pay if some strong ideas can be discovered among the mass of ideas generated by brainstorming. In a brainstorming session, one starts by defining the task. ("Our organization is trying to find ways to cut at least $100,000 from our training budget without diminishing our employees' levels of certifications. The goal of our group is to come up with some ways to do that.") One person is tasked to write down ideas so that everyone can see them. The rest of the participants are asked to throw out whatever ideas seem to come to mind. The sessions should be relatively short in order to keep energy levels high. A key rule is that any evaluation of any idea is to be deferred. ("Do not try to judge the merits of any idea.") The corollary is that personal comments or judgments are also forbidden. (The whole process loses its strength if participants feel mocked or scorned.) As the ideas are written down, participants will typically think of other ideas. The process builds on itself to create a substantial list of ideas. Those ideas can be evaluated later to discover what potentially viable options may have been created.

In 1985, Edward de Bono published "Six Thinking Hats: An Essential Approach to Business Management". The key idea in that book serves as a valuable tool to help generate novel options to be included in the decision making framework. De Bono's tool helps organizations to improve their insights into a situation by asking specific members of the organization or group to be responsible for taking a particular point of view when an issue is being considered. De Bono specifies six points of view, each represented by a "hat" the individual is asked to "wear". (The wearing of the hat is figurative, although some organizations actually use hats or tokens to indicate individual assignments in the process.)

The person wearing de Bono's blue hat is the control. This is the person who is focused on the thinking approach of the others. It is the person who seeks to keep the other people on task.

The white hat represents information and facts. The person with this hat is focused on what is known rather than on speculation.

The green hat represents the opposite of the white hat. It represents creativity. The person with this hat is asked to look for novel or different concepts.

The yellow hat stands for optimism. Its wearer looks deliberately for all of the positive aspects of the situation.

Conversely, the black hat stands for the negative side of things. The wearer of this hat is on the alert for trouble and problems. What are the bad possibilities or aspects of the situation?

The red hat represents emotions and feelings. The wearer is asked to be intuitive and emotional as the situation is assessed or considered.

People who are asked to "role play" a perspective or attitude are free to speak without fear that their words will be seen to reflect on their actual attitudes. Thus, a black hat wearer can voice objections and point to problems without being seen as an obstructionist. A red hat wearer can offer emotional concerns that he or she might otherwise be uncomfortable presenting. Additionally, of course, "wearing" a particular hat charges a person to take special care to consider a particular aspect of a situation.

One can add to the Six Thinking Hats concept by including other points of view that are particularly important to the organization. For example, one could ask a participant to represent the point of view of foreign customers or suppliers or parents, etc.

The tool can be used in a variety of ways, but the essence remains the same: The organization expects to gain valuable insights because individuals are asked to look at a situation through specific lenses.

Brainstorming or "thinking hat sessions" or any other method can be used to generate the set of options that can be evaluated as one seeks to make a good decision.

Evaluating the Options

The next two steps in the decision making framework are to "Evaluate the Options" and then to "Select the Best Option". But wait! Are these really two independent steps? Isn't it expected that the evaluation of options will point to the best option? Indeed, the evaluation step and the selection step can often be intertwined or combined, particularly in relatively simple decisions or in circumstances where the evaluation process identifies one clearly superior option. Even so, it is helpful to keep a distinct step for selecting the best option. Such a distinct step emphasizes the paramount role and clear responsibility of the decision maker while emphasizing the supporting nature of any evaluation processes.

Many techniques have been proposed to help people evaluate the possible options in the decision making process. This section offers a representative set of those techniques.

➤ Pros and Cons – (List making):

One of the earliest decision making techniques is the listing of advantages and disadvantages concerning options.   List making prods the decision maker to consider the good and the bad, and it helps the decision maker remain aware of all the factors he or she has thought of. However, list making doesn't really help in the weighing of the factors and the evaluation of the options. One can see children using this technique to force a decision they favor by ensuring that the pros are more numerous than the cons for the option they favored at the beginning. (Actually, I have seen adults do the same thing.) If each item on the list carries the same weight, one can generate some particularly skewed outcomes. (As an example, I saw a company use a version of list making to evaluate several software packages that were candidates for a new Enterprise Resource Planning System. The operations team noted a negative concern about one possible system because it lacked the ability to conform to the company's customer pricing system. That negative was cancelled by a positive observation from the IT staff that the system offered a strong set of software management tools. The company wound up selecting that option, and it struggled horribly to cope with the fact that the new ERP system could not be made to conform to the company's business model.)

➤ Weighted Averages

A natural step beyond simple list making is the recognition that some items on the list are more important than others. (Recognizing this truth would have benefited the unfortunate company that wound up selecting an ineffective ERP system.) One can assign a "weight" to each element being evaluated so some elements will have a greater impact on the final decision than others. Here is a simple example:

Weighted Averages and the Intern Staffing Decision

DoGood.org is a not-for-profit organization intended to support Cancer research. It offers an undergraduate internship position at its lobbying office on K Street in Washington, D.C. After eliminating candidates who do not meet baseline requirements, it uses a rubric to rate the remaining candidates' essays, letters of recommendation and experience on a score of 0 to 10. It then uses a score sheet to evaluate the candidates.

Here is the score sheet for John Doe:

Name: John Doe

GPA _____3.6_____

GPA is measured on a four point scale. It can be converted to a 10 point scale by multiplying the GPA by 2.5

Converted GPA _____9_____ (3.6 x 2.5 = 9)

Essay Rating _____8___

Recommendation Rating _____10_____

Experience Rating _____2_____

Rating Element	Score	Weight Factor	Weighted Score
GPA	3.6		
Converted to 10 point scale	9	X 4	36
Essay	8	X 2	16
Recommendations	10	X 1	10
Experience	2	X 3	6
		Weighted Score >	**68**

Let's deconstruct the weighting. DoGood is using four elements in its evaluation. The first element, GPA, is scored on a scale of zero to four. The next three elements, essay, recommendation and experience, are scored using a rubric on a scale of one to ten. (Notice how important it is for the rubrics to be well constructed and properly followed). DoGood's first adjustment is to multiply the GPA by 2.5 to make the GPA reflect a ten point scale instead of a four point scale. The next step is to multiply each of the scores by a weight factor that corresponds to DoGood's preferences. In this case, Recommendations serve as a baseline weight of one. The Essay is twice as important, Experience is three times as important, and GPA is four times as important.

According to the weighting preferences established by DoGood, John Doe's final score of 68 indicates he is a stronger candidate than those with lower total weighted scores, but a weaker candidate than those with higher total weighted scores.

This technique is open to wide variation in order to conform to the preferences of the company or organization. It has the advantage of causing decision makers to decide on the comparative importance of elements before any specific option is being reviewed.

➤ Probability Weighting (Expected Outcomes):

Some decision making situations involve probabilities and outcomes. These situations lend themselves to a simple mathematical calculation.

For instance, assume that ProfitSeeker Inc. has an option to bid on a construction job in Germany. The Sales Manager at ProfitSeeker estimates there is a 10% chance the company will win the job and make $50,000 profit. There is a 20% chance the company could win the bid but only make $20,000. There is a 70% chance the company will lose the bid. The expected outcome of this situation is a profit of $9,000. Here is how that figure was calculated:

10% X $50,000 profit = $5,000
20% X $20,000 Profit = $4,000
70% X $0 Profit   = $0

The expected outcome is $9,000 profit. (Note the cost of bidding is not included.)

Some people find it odd to say the expected outcome is $9,000 profit when that wasn't even one of the possibilities. The expected outcome makes sense if you assume the method will be used frequently so the outcomes "average out".

24

➢ Rational Assessment

"Rational Assessment" is a technique that sounds wonderful. It emulates the scientific approach to learning. A decision maker who uses "rational assessment" intends to conduct a dispassionate and objective analysis of the options in order to determine their strengths and weaknesses. The problem, of course, is that the real world is so complex, and biases are often so subtle, that one person's rational assessment might arrive at very different conclusions from another person's rational assessment. (See Appendix A for the analogous problem of using the "rational approach" to evaluate public policy.)

In spite of the problems of complexity and biases, we can still acknowledge the desirability of assessing options with as much objectivity as we can and supporting assessments with sound measurements and appropriate data.

➢ The "Sunk Cost" Trap

We have considered several techniques and aspects of evaluating options as part of the decision making process. Before moving on to actually selecting an option, it is important to consider a common error called the "sunk cost" trap.

A "sunk cost" is a cost that was generated in the past. For example, if I bought a lawn mower last month for $250, the $250 cost is a "sunk cost". (I "sank" $250 into a lawn mower.) The expense has already happened, and I cannot change it.

Now let's imagine the lawn mower's engine failed so I must consider solutions to the problem. One solution is to spend $150 for a major repair. Another solution is to discard the broken $250 lawn mower and to buy a used lawn mower for $125. Let's assume the repaired lawn mower and the used lawn mower would be virtually identical in performance, so the deciding factor is cost. The amount I paid for the lawn mower really shouldn't be a factor, but it is often difficult to set aside such things as purchase prices. If I fall for the "sunk cost" trap, I will think the used lawn mower will cost me $375, (the $125 price plus throwing away the $250 lawn mower). Having fallen for the 'sunk cost" trap, I will incorrectly decide to spend $150 to repair the broken lawn mower. What I should do is to recognize it will be cheaper to buy the used lawn mower for $125 in order to have a functioning lawn mower in the garage. I do not need to consider what I paid for the broken lawn mower. The "sunk cost" of $250 doesn't matter.

Here is another illustration of the "sunk costs" trap. An investor owns 100 shares of Widget Corporation. The investor knows the market price today is $12 a share. The investor is worried that competitors are attracting market share away from Widget Corp. which might drive the market price down. As the investor tries to decide to sell shares or to hold shares, should he or she want to know the price of the shares when they were purchased? No. A proper assessment only considers the expectation about the future price of the stock. Selling at $12 today or holding at $12 today is a decision that is unrelated to the purchase price of the stock. Even so, many investors would be reluctant to sell if they had paid $15 a share, and many would be happy to sell if they had paid $10 a share. They are falling into the "sunk cost" trap. (Please note this example sets aside any considerations of capital gains taxes.)

The "sunk cost" trap is real and vicious. It clouds our assessments by inducing us to include costs (in time and money) that have already been paid and cannot be changed. To avoid falling for the "sunk cost" trap, only evaluate situations based on "forward-looking" streams of money or time.

The rule is: <u>Sunk Costs Don't Count</u>.

Selecting the Best Option (Making the Decision)

Once the options have been assessed or evaluated, it is time to make the decision. (See the end of this section for a refinement about when to make the decision.) Note that assessment and evaluation assist the decision maker, but they do not replace the decision maker. The decision maker bears the responsibility for the decision.

How is the decision maker to decide? While it is tempting to argue the assessments are strong instruments pointing to the best choice among competing options, most decisions of serious complexity must be made by people, not by systems. The decision maker brings experience and insight to the task of making a decision. Decision makers also bring fears, personal factors and extraneous concerns to the process. The best a decision maker can do is to be aware of the various influences as he or she considers the options and makes a choice. Here are three concepts and tools to help the decision maker in this task. They are Intuition, Even Swaps and Voting.

➢ Intuition

When it comes down to it, most decisions are probably made on the basis of intuition. Ideally, this intuition is

28

more than a mystical preference. Intuition is influenced by the experiences, training and perceptions (conscious and subconscious) of the decision maker. An informed "gut feel" is often the strongest mechanism for making a choice. (In fact, a theory of management, called "Management by Walking Around", is based on taking steps to help the manager gain the subtle experiences and insights that will help to develop good instincts and intuition.) Caution: Recognizing the role of intuition in decision making can create a trap. It can lead decision makers to avoid the hard work of serious assessment of options. ("After all, if the decision boils down to intuition, why bother with all of the effort to fiddle with weighted averages, etc.?") Remember that the final decision should be supported by the assessments and tools used to help a decision maker and also by a decision maker's awareness of factors beyond formal assessments.

As General, and later Secretary of State, Colin Powell wrote:

> Use the formula P 40 to 70, in which P stands for the probability of success and the numbers indicate the percentage of information acquired. Once the information is in the 40 to 70 range, go with your gut. Don't take action if you have only enough information to give you less than a 40

percent chance of being right, but don't wait until you have enough facts to be 100 percent sure, because by then it is almost always too late. Today, excessive delays in the name of information-gathering breeds "analysis paralysis." Procrastination in the name of reducing risk actually increases risk.

(From Powell, C. (Date uncertain) A Leadership Primer, Retrieved from http://www.think-energy.net/Colin-Powell-on-Leadership.pdf March 2016)

For additional ideas about trusting your instincts, see the Beaton article at Appendix B.

You may also want to read the thoughts about going with your gut from Jack Welch former CEO of GE: https://www.linkedin.com/pulse/20131112125301-86541065-when-to-go-with-your-gut

As an aside, please do not focus too closely on exact percentages. After all, you are unlikely to really know precise probabilities of success or absolute measures of all possible information. Accept the general idea that, at some point, you will have almost all of the information you can reasonably gather, so it is time to make a decision.

➢ Even Swaps

Recall the techniques used to assess options. Notice how the techniques require some sort of outside information about priorities and values. For example, the intern staffing decision showed that experience was to be weighted with a factor of three while the candidate's essay carried a factor of two. Those weighting factors are critical to the technique, but where did those factors come from? Well, they came from the judgment of the person or people who created the weighting scale. That judgement was condensed into a set of seemingly-precise quantitative factors, but the precision is just an illusion. We have to remember that weighting factors simply reflect an effort to move from fuzzy notions about what sorts of things are important to a more concrete expression of those fuzzy notions.

Condensing fuzzy notions and preferences into quantitative factors works generally well for a process to be used to assess multiple alternatives, such as candidates for an intern position, or to provide structure to decisions that have to be made by different decision makers over time. However, what about a decision that will not become part of a repeated or routine process? Can such a decision also be supported with a bit more formality that draws out the preferences and priorities of the institution? The answer is yes, and the technique is called Even Swaps.

Even Swaps is a decision making technique that uses the priorities of an institution (as expressed by its leaders) to establish one-time, imaginary trade-offs among options to boil a set of options down to a single best choice.

The idea of Even Swaps comes from Hammond, Keeney and Raiffa in their March 1998 Harvard Business Review article entitled *Even Swaps: A Rational Method for Making Trade-offs.* (It can be found at https://hbr.org/1998/03/even-swaps-a-rational-method-for-making-trade-offs.) The following section presents the ideas and some thoughts about the article. An example is also provided.

The essential idea about Even Swaps is the idea of making balanced trade-offs between unlike factors. It is easy to choose if you have only one factor. (I want to buy a new charger for my cell phone. Which option is cheapest?) However, more complex decisions involve multiple factors, and the relative values of those factors are rarely evident. (This used car has a dent. That used car is the wrong color. The third option is a car that has high mileage.)

How can you make a wise and well-informed decision involving multiple and complex trade-offs? Even Swaps offers a technique to help.

Creating the Consequences Table:

The first step in even Swaps is to create what Hammond, Keeney and Raiffa call a "consequences table". A "consequences table" is simply a matrix with a row for each objective (or decision factor) and a column for each alternative (or option).

Here is an example for choosing among graduate school choices:

Objectives	Option A	Option B	Option C	Option D	Option E
Net cost per year	$55,000	$39,000	$37,000	$34,000	$26,000
Location	Poor	Great	OK	OK	Great
Reputation	Very Strong	Adequate	Strong	Strong	Adequate
Quality of life	Good	Excellent	Adequate	Excellent	Adequate
Time required	24 months	24 months	24 months	24 months	18 months

IMPORTANT: Take time to get the consequences table right. (As they say with computers, "garbage in = garbage out".) It is vital to include all of the important factors (objectives) in the table. Note the table doesn't include options that were ruled out right from the start, such as options without the right academic program or options with poor reputations.

Eliminating "Dominated" Alternatives:

Once you have a good consequences table, you can examine the alternatives to see if any alternative is clearly inferior to a different alternative. In the example, you can see Option C is worse or the same as Option D in all objectives. Option D dominates Option C, so Option C can be eliminated from consideration.

The revised table looks like this:

Objectives	Option A	Option B	Option D	Option E
Net cost per year	$55,000	$39,000	$34,000	$26,000
Location	Poor	Great	OK	Great
Reputation	Very Strong	Adequate	Strong	Adequate
Quality of life	Good	Excellent	Excellent	Adequate
Time required	24 months	24 months	24 months	18 months

34

At this point, the originators of Even Swaps go on to talk about the concept of "practical dominance" which means an alternative is worse or no better than another alternative in all objectives except perhaps for a small advantage in a minor objective. In such a case, the originators argue the alternative can also be eliminated. I choose to omit this step as there is often room for debate about the judgment call, and omitting the step causes no real problems.

Creating The Ranking Table ????

Hammond, Keeney and Raiffa note some consequences tables can be extensive and, therefore, confusing. They argue one can add clarity by converting the ratings of the objectives into numerical rankings. While I agree a ranking table adds clarity, I suggest one avoid the use of a ranking table as the conversion of ratings into rankings can obscure valuable information. For example, here is the ranking table for our example:

Ranking Table – Graduate School Decision

Objectives	Option A	Option B	Option D	Option E
Net cost per year	4	3	2	1
Location	3	1	2	1
Reputation	1	3	2	3
Quality of life	2	1	1	3
Time required	2	2	2	1

According to the rankings, the *net cost per year* for Option D is one level worse than Option E just as Option A's *net cost per year* is one level worse than Option B. However, the dollar differences in those variations are not at all the same. Accordingly, I do not recommend using a ranking table unless the situation is quite confusing. In addition, should you choose to use a ranking table, it is wise to revert to the original consequences table once you start to generate an Even Swap.

Generating the Even Swap

Creating the "even swap" is the heart of the Even Swaps technique. The idea is to try to make imaginary paired changes (swaps or trades) between objective consequences so that all options wind up having the same consequence (actual or imaginary). That objective can then be eliminated from consideration.

Here is how to do it with our example:

Let's look at the "time required" objective. Three of the remaining options in the table require 24 months. One requires 18 months. Let's make some imaginary changes in the consequences table so all options seem to require 24 months. No changes are required for Options A, B and D. Changing Option E's measure of time required from 18 to 24 months would make all options have the same measure. However, doing so would be to the disadvantage of Option E, so we must compensate Option E by giving it an imaginary advantage in some other objective. Let's use the cost objective for the imaginary compensation. How much is it worth to you to have a program finish in 18 months instead of 24 months? After considering the effect of raises and time, you decide the 6 months difference is worth $5,000 in Net Annual Cost. In such a case, you could subtract an imaginary $5,000 from the Net Annual Cost of Option E. The consequences table now looks like this:

Objectives	Option A	Option B	Option D	Option E
Net cost per year	$55,000	$39,000	$34,000	~~$26,000~~ $21,000
Location	Poor	Great	OK	Great
Reputation	Very Strong	Adequate	Strong	Adequate
Quality of life	Good	Excellent	Excellent	Adequate
Time required	24 months	24 months	24 months	~~18 months~~ 24 months

The "Time Required" objective is now identical across all objectives, so it can be dropped from the table leaves a revised table like this:

Objectives	Option A	Option B	Option D	Option E
Net cost per year	$55,000	$39,000	$34,000	$21,000
Location	Poor	Great	OK	Great
Reputation	Very Strong	Adequate	Strong	Adequate
Quality of life	Good	Excellent	Excellent	Adequate

We are making progress. The table is smaller. We should now check to see if there is any "Dominance" to be seen in the new table. (Does any option do as well or better in all objectives compared against another option? If so, the inferior option may be eliminated from consideration.) We see no dominance in this situation, so now it is time for another swap.

Let's look at the *quality of life* objective. We will make imaginary swaps in Options A and E so all options have a consequence of "excellent" in quality of life. Dong so, of course, means Options A and E would enjoy an imaginary boost to their ratings, so we will also have to "even things out" by assigning an imaginary disadvantage elsewhere.

The originators of Even Swaps suggest we might try to make trade-offs in any other objective. For instance, we might drop Option E's location consequence from "Great" to "OK" to balance increasing its quality of life rating to "Excellent". I disagree. While it is possible for such swaps to be evenly balanced, I think it is unlikely. Instead, I urge people using Even Swaps always to use the cost objective in order to make the balancing swap. Virtually all decisions, certainly in business or government, involve costs, so a cost objective should always be present. Using cost as a balancing factor is clear and leads the decision maker to make more clearly defined judgment calls.

Let's go to the decision maker and ask, "How much would you be willing to pay for an "excellent" quality of life rating instead of an "adequate" or "good" rating?" The decision maker has to scratch his or her head and decide. Let's assume the answer is that an excellent rating instead of a good rating is worth $1,500 per year and an excellent rating instead of an adequate rating is worth $4,000 per year. We can make those imaginary changes and produce the following consequences table:

Objectives	Option A	Option B	Option D	Option E
Net cost per year	~~$55,000~~ $56,500	$39,000	$34,000	~~$21,000~~ $25,000
Location	Poor	Great	OK	Great
Reputation	Very Strong	Adequate	Strong	Adequate
Quality of life	~~Good~~ Excellent	Excellent	Excellent	~~Adequate~~ Excellent

Notice the imaginary improvements in the *quality of life* objective were offset by imaginary disadvantages in the *cost per year* objective. The *quality of life* objective is now the same across all options, so it can be eliminated.

Objectives	Option A	Option B	Option D	Option E
Net cost per year	$56,500	$39,000	$34,000	$25,000
Location	Poor	Great	OK	Great
Reputation	Very Strong	Adequate	Strong	Adequate

It is time to check for dominance again. Note that Option E dominates Option B, so Option B can be eliminated.

Objectives	Option A	Option D	Option E
Net cost per year	$56,500	$34,000	$25,000
Location	Poor	OK	Great
Reputation	Very Strong	Strong	Adequate

Our next swap should be in the objective, *reputation.* Once again, we have to ask the decision maker an important question; "How much would you pay per year to attend a school with a "Very Strong" reputation instead of a reputation that is merely "Strong" or "Adequate"? Suppose the decision maker says, "I would pay an extra $6,000 a year for a school with a very strong reputation instead of a just a strong reputation, and I would pay an extra $15,000 a year for a school with a strong reputation instead of merely an adequate one." (From the answer, we can tell a very strong reputation is worth $21,000 more per year than an adequate reputation.) With this information, we can make our swaps.

Objectives	Option A	Option D	Option E
Net cost per year	$56,500	~~$34,000~~ $40,000	~~$25,000~~ $46,000
Location	Poor	OK	Great
Reputation	Very Strong	~~Strong~~ Very Strong	~~Adequate~~ Very Strong

The objective, *reputation*, has now been equalized, so it is eliminated from consideration.

Objectives	Option A	Option D	Option E
Net cost per year	$56,500	$40,000	$46,000
Location	Poor	OK	Great

Checking for dominance, we see both Options D and E dominate Option A, so Option A is eliminated.

Objectives	Option D	Option E
Net cost per year	$40,000	$46,000
Location	OK	Great

We are down to our final swap. We ask the decision maker how much he would pay per year to be in a great location instead of merely an OK location. Suppose the answer is "I will be busy with my studies, so location is not critical. I would pay $2,000 a year for a great location instead of an OK location."

The new table looks like this:

Objectives	Option D	Option E
Net cost per year	$42,000	$46,000
Location	Great	Great

The new consequences table offers us the suggested decision to select Option D.

Note the adjective "suggested". The Even Swaps method doesn't force a decision maker to agree. The method merely highlighted specific trade-offs and led the decision maker to assign weights to those trade-offs. Remember as well that nothing was really changed.

Let's go back to the original consequences table.

Objectives	Option A	Option B	Option C	Option D	Option E
Net cost per year	$55,000	$39,000	$37,000	$34,000	$25,000
Location	Poor	Great	OK	OK	Great
Reputation	Very Strong	Adequate	Strong	Strong	Adequate
Quality of life	Good	Excellent	Adequate	Excellent	Adequate
Time required	24 months	24 months	24 months	24 months	18 months

The Even Swaps technique has led us to the conclusion that Option D is the preferred choice. It is now time for the decision maker to perform a sort of "sanity check". How does the decision maker feel about the outcome? If the decision maker is uncomfortable about the outcome, then he or she should ask why. What factors were not included? Were any of the weighting choices skewed? Answers to those questions could cause the decision maker to revise the Even Swaps process by adding overlooked objectives or by seeking better evaluation and weighting judgments. Remember, we are trying to arrive at the best decision, not impose a decision based on the mechanics of the Even Swaps method. The final "sanity check" is an important component of reaching the decision.

The example above had a single decision maker wrestling with a relatively clear problem. Organizations may confront more complex problems with a variety of subordinate decision makers involved in setting the stage for a final decision. In such a case, Even Swaps possesses the additional virtue of causing us to identify the person in the organization who is best suited to make the judgement calls about consequences and about the weighting of swaps.

As Hammond, Keeney and Raiffa summarize:
   A. One should make the easiest swaps first in order to clarify the situation prior to confronting "swaps" whose relative values are more difficult to assign. ("Easy" swaps are swaps which seem to have straight–forward values associated with the exchanges.)
   B. One should concentrate on the amount of each swap and not be distracted by the perceived importance of the objective.
   C. Swaps are supposed to be consistent. (If moving from "excellent" to "good" in a given objective is

exchanged for $10,000 in one option, moving from "excellent" to "good" in the given objective should be exchanged for $10,000 in any other option.)

D. One should always seek out information or better informed evaluators in order to make informed swaps.

Whew! Even Swaps seems complicated. Of course, it is, as techniques go, but it is simple in concept. Even Swaps requires us to make balancing judgements about the competing factors that differentiate one option from another. Done well, Even Swaps will bring to the surface stark challenges as we seek to discover just how much we prefer one level of a decision factor over another. Even if you do not do a full and formal Even Swaps, the concept is useful.

> Voting

Another way to try to choose among competing options is to vote. Voting, done well, tries to take advantage of "the wisdom of crowds". (For additional details, see *Surowiecki, J. (2005). The wisdom of crowds. New York: Anchor Books.*) Voting is a simple way to express the preference of a group. If the group consists of people who are seriously invested in the decision and who are well informed, at least about part of the situation, then we assume voting will generate a valuable outcome. Of course, voting can also be a way to dodge a tough question and to avoid responsibility. If you choose to use voting to make a tough decision, ensure you do so in the expectation that the voters will make a collective choice that is expected to be better than the choice of some other expert or boss.

> ➤ A Consideration of Timing and Sufficient Information

At this point, we have considered several ways to handle the task of evaluating options and making the choice among competing options. Before we leave the "Selecting the Best Option" and move on to "Defining Success or Failure", we should pause to consider the timing of making a decision. You see, in the real world, not all decisions are forced upon you. Sometimes it is up to you or to your organization to determine when to deal with a situation, solve a problem, or make a decision. "Deciding when to decide" can be quite a puzzle, and the challenge is compounded by the reality that you will almost never have all of the information you would like to have. The trap you want to avoid is allowing uncertainty to freeze you in place.

Given that you will rarely have all of the information you would like to have, it is important to get used to the idea of making a decision in the face of substantial uncertainty. Study the situation and decide if you can reasonably get valuable information in a correct time frame. Take steps to do so if you can. If it is not likely you will be able to gain much additional information, then it would be a mistake to delay.

It is tempting to rationalize indecision by saying something like: "Darn. I cannot be sure I am making the correct decision. Perhaps the situation will become clearer if I postpone making a decision now." Committees and teams will often stall in this way. Here is a technique to help you: If someone at a meeting suggests postponing a decision or action until the next meeting, ask yourself what you expect to learn or do between now and the next meeting. Who will do what to enrich the decision making process at the next meeting? Without a set of solid answers to those questions, the delay is probably just a rationalization to avoid choosing or acting now.

The previous section of the book covered the step in the rational decision making sequence called "Select the Best Option". That section was long, so here is a reminder of where we are in the decision making sequence.

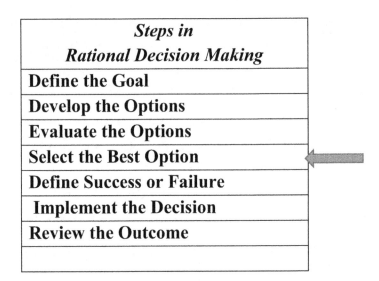

Steps in Rational Decision Making
Define the Goal
Develop the Options
Evaluate the Options
Select the Best Option
Define Success or Failure
Implement the Decision
Review the Outcome

"Define Success or Failure" is the next step in our discussion of the rational decision making process.

Defining Success or Failure

It is tempting to think the hard work has been done once a decision has been reached. Actually, there is still plenty to do. The next significant, and often overlooked, step is to define success or failure. How will you know if the decision is well-implemented and getting the job done? What measurements will you use? When will you measure? What values do you expect the measurements to register? What actions will you take if the measurements come up short? If things are not going well, how will you know if the problem is the decision, the implementation, or both?

This step is powerful. People sometimes let their egos become attached to a decision. Alternatively, people sometimes just operate on auto-pilot and keep working without checking the level of success or failures. One may waste far too many resources trying to force a success when the best thing to do is to cut losses and rethink the problem. Deliberately including the definition of success or failure in the decision making process helps to avoid the problems of egos and auto-pilot.

Some stock traders do a very good job of including this step in their decision making processes. The trader might decide to "Buy XYZ at $40" because the trader anticipates the stock will rise. However, at the same time, the trader might issue a "stop loss" order directing the stock broker to "Sell XYZ if the stock falls to $37". In effect, the trader is saying, "My analysis tells me XYZ will rise in value, but I might be wrong, so I should define failure now and cut my losses before I lose too much."

McNaughton-McKay Electric Company of Georgia offers a strong example of the value of "Defining Success of Failure" as part of its decision to open a new branch store. The General Manager looked at the available information and anticipated the opening of a new branch would increase profits. However, he also took the effort to define the expected increases in sales and profits that would define success or failure. He established an expected range of sales and profit numbers for the first five years. Some ranges of numbers would mark a clear success. Some ranges would mark disappointing results but still justify keeping the branch open. Finally, some ranges would be indications of failure and would trigger closing the branch. The initial performance resulted in measurements that justified continuing the effort after the first year, but, in spite of plenty of hard work during the next couple of years, the required increases in sales and profit levels were not reached. A major assessment of the situation found that the added costs of the branch were not justified by sufficient increases in sales and profits. Accordingly, the branch was closed. The General Manager had been enthusiastic about the prospects of the new branch. (It is possible the enthusiasm may have put a rosy glow on some of the initial assessments.) Absent a proper definition of success or failure, the General Manager might have fallen into the trap of throwing good money after bad in the desperate hope to protect his ego. However, because the General Manager included the definition of success or failure in his decision making process, he was able to say, in effect, "Well, we recognized the risk at the start of the decision to open the branch. It was a proper trial, but, the results failed to meet the goals we established. Closing the branch is the right thing to do and is in keeping with the evaluation factors we defined as part of our decision to try establishing the new branch."

Implementing the Decision

Once a decision has been made, an organization faces the obvious next step of implementing the decision. The decision must be communicated, plans must be made, responsibilities and duties must be assigned, resources must be allocated, and actions must be taken. At this stage, one can see that "decision making" has crossed the boundary into "management and leadership". Still, it is important to keep "implementing the decision" as a step in the decision making process for two reasons. The first reason is related to simplicity and feasibility. Acknowledging one will have to implement a decision helps decision makers remember to select options that are "doable" rather than options that would be awkward or even impossible to put into place. The second reason is related to inertia. In too many organizations, the connection between deciding and doing is unclear or weak. Including "implementing the decision" as a step in the process helps to remind organizations to push the decision out into the "real world" of action.

Review the Outcome

The job is not quite finished once the decision has been put into effect. We still need to evaluate the success or failure of the decision and its implementation. Go back to the step where we "defined success or failure". Make the defined measurements and then ask "what is happening?"

If the measurements are positive, and the situation seems normal, then it is reasonable to declare victory. The decision was made. The implementation phase is over. The situation is good. Consign the issue to normal management and move on. (If the issue was major, or if you expect to see a similar situation in the future, it is probably a good idea to write up some "lessons learned" and archive the process for future use.)

However, if the measurements are not positive, then work remains to be done. Assess the situation. What is not working well? Why? Perhaps the decision itself was flawed, and a different decision should be adopted and implemented. Perhaps the decision was a good one, (it had the best chance of success), but the situation is still bad, so something else must be done. Perhaps the problem is centered on faulty implementation rather than a faulty decision. In any case, you are stuck with a bad situation and must take steps to find and implement a solution. Record any "lessons learned", and go back to the beginning of your problem solving and decision making processes in order to find a new path forward.

III.   Decision Making in Organizations.

In addition to taking steps to gain an understanding of decision making in general, scholars and practitioners of management also want to understand how organizations approach decision making. What structures, methods and techniques do organizations use to arrive at major decisions for the organization as a whole? What generally works, and what does not? As you can imagine, organizations will try to take advantage of the concepts associated with decision making in general, and they will hope also to take advantage of the resources available to organizations. In addition, organizations will have to deal with bureaucratic or structural issues ranging from the straight-forward issues of recording and communicating decisions to the incredibly complex and troublesome issues of power, accountability, risk avoidance, blame avoidance, corporate politics, etc.

Some organizations approach decision making by just relying on the boss (the CEO or General Manager or President) to make decisions for the organization. While such an approach has the advantages of simplicity and clear accountability, the approach fails to take advantage of other strengths or assets in the organization. In addition, relying only on the boss creates room for a sense of arbitrariness, and it misses the opportunity to develop a sense of shared purpose and mutual commitment among the members of the organization.

Accordingly, many organizations have adopted methods, some of them highly structured and formal, to tap into the resources of the organization as it seeks to make important decisions. Generally speaking, these methods are based on the rational approach to decision making. They expect an organization should be able to draw on its resources to create a clear definition of the issue, a strong set of viable alternative solutions, rich and insightful evaluations of those alternative solutions, and a careful, clear and fully-communicated decision. Virtually all methods of organizational decision making also have the additional benefit of providing a lasting record of what was decided and when it was decided.

There are, as one would expect, many ideas about how organizations can or should approach decision making. Of course, the expectation of excellent decision making by organizations is only an ideal. In reality, organizational decision making is complicated and weakened by internal politics, bureaucratic concerns and communication difficulties. These issues are in addition to the normal issues that plague any form of decision making, organizational or otherwise.

Let's look at two examples of organizational decision making. First, we will take a glance at the highly structured decision making process used in the US Army. Second, we will see a real case to show how even a careful decision making structure is not sufficient to guarantee good decisions.

The US Army Decision Briefing

The US Army offers a course to train officers to serve in staff positions. The course, called the Combined Arms and Services Staff School, or CAS3, includes instruction in the preparation and presentation of a decision briefing. The structure of the briefing illustrates the Army's approach to decision making.

A staff supports a commander in many ways. One role of a staff is to support the commander by assessing a situation or problem and recommending a course of action to be taken. The staff engages in decision making analysis and recommends a course of action (a choice) to the commander. A decision briefing is presented to a commander to inform the commander of the work of the staff and to seek the commander's approval or disapproval of a recommended course of action.

The format of a decision briefing illustrates how the US Army has embraced the rational decision making process and supported it with structured coordination and input in order to arrive at decisions for the organization. The next section shows the format of the US Army's decision briefing by listing the order of slides to be used in the presentation of a decision briefing.

US Army Decision Briefing Format

Cover Slide
Purpose
Problem
Recommendation
Prior Coordination (with concurrence or non-concurrence)
    Outline of the Briefing Body
Background
Facts Bearing on the Problem
Assumptions
Discussion
Courses of Action (COA) (Alternatives)
Screening Criteria
Screened out Courses of Action
Surviving Courses of Action
Evaluation Criteria
Priority of Criteria
Analysis
Comparison of Courses of Action
Conclusion
Recommendation
    Backup Slides
Raw Data Matrix
Weighting of Criteria
Decision Matrix
Sensitivity Analysis

The information about the Us Army decision briefing process comes from:
http://8tharmy.korea.army.mil/501MI/content/CAS3StaffOfficer Guide.pdf

As you can see, a staff officer following this format will have to coordinate with others in order to clearly identify the problem and identify possible solutions. Then the staff officer will have to develop the set of criteria to be used to evaluate the possible solutions, gather information, apply the criteria, compare the solutions and offer a recommendation which includes agreement and disagreement from key individuals or agencies. The commander must take responsibility for approving the decision, but one can see the commander was supported by a process designed to take advantage of the assets of the organization while applying the rational decision making approach.

Please note the US Army's decision making approach is only one of many organizational approaches. You might want to look at Appendix C to read some thoughts about how the German Army's approach to decision making is qualitatively different.

The Failure at "AnyCo"

The previous section illustrated one of the ways an organization, (in this case the US Army), can rely on a carefully structured way to incorporate rational decision making into its corporate decision making. The next section will offer an example of a decision making failure largely caused by blind adherence to a methodology.

A large company, let's call it "AnyCo", had been relying on a privately written computer program to run the organization. The enterprise management software program handled everything: Accounting and finance, billing, customer management, vendor management, sales, inventory control, shipping, etc. Recognizing the software was past its prime, difficult to alter, and totally dependent on the knowledge of one person, AnyCo's board decided it was time to consider adopting a commercial enterprise management software system.

AnyCo tasked one of its key managers to lead a search for suitable software programs. That search leader recognized the need to communicate with each of the managers of various parts of the organization in order to define the specific capacities and characteristics required of the new ERP system. (Thus, the search leader was embracing the rational approach and attempting to offer a detailed definition of the goal.)

The many departments and subordinate parts of AnyCo generated an extensive list of demands and expectations about what the new system should be able to do.

Having developed a set of possible commercial ERP systems that might work, the leader of the search was ready to move into the evaluation phase. The leader gathered information about costs, customer reviews, program capacities, corporate claims, etc. associated with each candidate system. The mass of information was daunting, but it served to narrow the search down to three possible candidates.

A committee of key managers and corporate leaders debated the three choices and was unable to arrive at a consensus about which system would be best. Therefore, the search leader chose to use a combination of weighted average and voting to arrive at a decision. The manager developed a score card with weights and asked each key manager to rate all three candidate systems within the key manager's area of responsibility. Here is a glimpse of what parts of the completed scorecard looked like:

Rate each candidate system on a scale of 0-10 with 10 being best.

Rated Area		Candidate A	B	Candidate C
(by CFO)				
Financial Mgmt.	Score	5	6	5
	Weight	X2	X2	X2
	Result	10	12	10

(Note: This is just an illustration, not an actual copy of what was used.)

The search leader collected all of the score cards, summed the results, and arrived at a total score for each candidate. The committee of managers, frustrated by their inability to arrive at a consensus, and eager to resolve the problem, selected the candidate with the highest score and recommended its adoption.

But wait! Some of the managers were surprised at the result and checked the details. They saw that one key manager had an astonishing score card. It looked something like this:

Rated Area		Candidate A	B	Candidate C
(By IT Mgr)				
Information Technology	Score	1	10	1
	Weight	X2	X2	X2
	Result	2	20	2

Notice, the IT Manager used a rating system that was binary. The manager used only two ratings, all or almost nothing. As a result, that manager's scores dominated the scores from other managers who had rated the candidate systems more evenly.

The search leader might have recognized a weakness in training the key managers in the expectations about scoring, and might have decided to repeat the process after some sharing of scoring mindsets. However, the decision making process had already consumed months of time and effort. Everyone was tired and frustrated. The search leader presented the findings, and AnyCo signed a contract with the winning candidate.

Sadly, the story has an unhappy ending. The selected system, while strong in IT, failed to perform in other critical areas. AnyCo lost $10 million and adopted a different ERP system.

The point of the story is to highlight how personalities, politics, weariness, pressure, lack of training, or other factors can be obstacles to decision making by organizations. Formal decision making methods can sometimes serve to mask, but not counter, such obstacles. Corporate decision makers should remember that tools and decision making methods are only guides and supports.

IV. Next Steps in Understanding Decision Making

So far we have considered conditions associated with decision making as well as some concepts and techniques associated with decision making. There are certainly many other ways of looking at the same elements, and we can be confident new ideas and new decision making methods will be presented in the future. We know decision making is imperfect, so it makes sense to keep seeking even slightly better ways to arrive at decisions having a higher probability of leading to good outcomes.

V.   *Conclusion*

Real decisions, rather than simple choices or preferences, involve uncertainty. We have considered some methods to help make decisions that have the best chance of success, but we also recognize we cannot guarantee success. Therefore, good decision making includes provisions for the possibility of a bad outcome.

Because serious decision making can be difficult and time-consuming, and because there are no techniques that are certain to reach the best decision, some leaders can be tempted to forego the hard work and jump into simply making a choice. At the other extreme, some leaders can be tempted to add even more complexity and formality to the decision making process in order to spread the blame or to embrace the false hope that more complexity will lead to better decisions. Skillful leaders will seek to avoid those two extremes, and they will also coach their subordinates to avoid the extremes, to learn to make better decisions and to be agile and flexible in the face of uncertainty.

Decisions get made, or not, one way or another. Many theorists recognize the huge advantage one could gain by making even a marginal improvement in the quality of decision making. Accordingly, there are many theories about how we can improve our decision making styles and approaches. Please do not try to chase the latest decision making fads. Instead, look at each new theory you encounter and adopt what seems valuable to you. Look at the outcomes of your decisions. Evaluate the quality of your decision making. Learn from your mistakes and learn from your successes.

It is also important to recognize types of decisions. Some decisions are small (of little consequence) such as the decision about the type of file cabinet to purchase for one office. Other decisions, of course, can be major, such as the decision about where to build a new facility. Obviously, we want to spend our precious attention units and time on the significant decisions.

Decisions can deal with "one-off" (one time) situations, or they can be deal with systemic or repeated matters. One-off situations simply require solutions that work. Situations that are likely to be repeated merit additional attention. The chosen solution for a repeating situation must not only work, it must work well enough to be converted into a normal business practice that can be taught to the staff and followed. (When I ran an electric parts distribution business, I noticed my employees frequently ran into the problem of what to do when a customer ordered something we did not routinely offer for sale. We developed a standard solution (a process) to address that circumstance.)

Decision-making is an art. Yes, we can support our decision-making with good numbers-crunching and scientific analysis, but we always face some degree of uncertainty. That means some of our decisions will have bad outcomes. We should plan on that. Once you have made a decision and are ready to implement it, ask yourself questions such as:

How will I know the decision was a good one?
How will I know if the implementation is working or not?
What are my fallback options?
What should trigger the use of a fallback option?

Finally, consider the overlap between planning and decision making. One can say that decision making applied to future actions equals planning.

VI. Appendices

Appendix A – Rational Approach

Students of Business and Public Policy at Young Harris College are asked to consider how various public policy options or decisions can be evaluated. The "Rational Approach" defines one of those evaluation methods used in the analysis of public policy. The following passage illustrates how the Rational Approach is supposed to work and also shows how the "Incremental Approach" (sometimes called the "Humble Approach") arises in response to some of the real-world difficulties of using the Rational Approach in the analysis of public policy. The passage is offered to help students see similar problems and responses in the use of Rational Assessment of options in decision making

"The Rational Approach to public policy analysis": The scientific method paved the way for huge advances. The logic and rigor of the scientific method hold powerful appeal. The social sciences lack the "repeatability" of the hard sciences, so efforts to adapt the scientific method to the social sciences have been frustrating. Still, the appeal is there. Accordingly, social scientists, (and public policy analysts broadly belong in that category), seek a rigorous and "scientific" approach to the analysis of public policy. (The lure of "positivism" is strong.) The rational approach to policy analysis is the result. It requires the analyst to examine public policy using logic, facts, and reason in a clearly defined set of steps. (Careful here. There is no single "rational approach." Academicians love to alter or to modify theories. Accordingly, one could, no doubt, discover a variety of sets of steps to be taken during "rational analysis." I will present a simple set of steps common to most varieties of rational analysis.)

The Steps in the Rational Approach:

>Identify the issue.
>Identify the goals and how to measure them
>Develop several possible paths (alternatives) to the goals
>Evaluate the alternatives. (This is easy to say, but hard to do. Generally, this step will include a cost-benefit analysis and a deliberate effort to anticipate unintended consequences.)
>Choose an alternative
>Implement the alternative. (This step is generally outside of the hands of the analysts, but it is still part of the process.)
>Evaluate the results.

"The Incremental or "Humble" Approach: If you follow all of the steps in the rational approach, you will frequently get to the evaluation stage and say, "Rats! We didn't really hit the target." So, the process starts over as you try to steer the outcomes of the policy closer to the goal. The Incremental Approach argues that such a situation is to be expected. Large and complex policy issues are just plain beyond our ability to "solve" correctly with one iteration of the rational approach. Accordingly, proponents of the Incremental Approach favor taking small steps followed by adjustments to those steps as one seeks to reach the goals. It is a deliberately "humble" approach in that it recognizes we are not able to create a fully effective policy right at the start. The approach values pilot programs and respects the advantage that we enjoy in the USA because our states often employ a variety of different approaches to solve similar problems.

(The passage above comes from "Business and Public Policy" by John Van Vliet pp. 60-62.)

Appendix B

"Trust Your Gut and Make Better Decisions"
Margaret Beaton 27 January 2015

Reprinted here with permission from
Dr. Margaret Beaton.

How often has someone said to you 'Trust your gut'? Do you? Or do you go through a logical analysis of the pros and cons of every major decision you make?

Being urged to trust your gut is the same as being urged to listen to your inner voice, act on your hunch, let your intuition decide, and follow your sixth sense. These interchangeable colloquialisms refer to allowing your heart to rule your head in making decisions. I often advise my clients to do just this. Here's why.

Authors ranging from US organizational theorist Warren Bennis in *On Becoming a Leader* to German neuroscientist Gerd Gigerenzer in *Gut Feelings*, have written about the scientific evidence that shows trusting your gut is more often than not the right thing to do – and a complement to the rational process of systematic analysis prior to making a decision.

Trust your gut Susan!
Susan trusted her gut. And she has never looked back.

On the fast track to the top echelons of management in the inner government department where she had worked for nine years, Susan faced a big career decision. She could continue to wait for a long-serving colleague to be moved on which would pave the way for her promotion into the department's executive suite. Or she could accept an offer to be deputy chief executive of a small government agency – and be a contender for its top job within a year.

A trained mathematician, Susan meticulously built decision-trees and applied game theory to the decision she faced. Whichever way she looked at the options, or her friends advised her, staying put and waiting had the lower short-term risk and greater certainty of ultimate success. Yet Susan felt uncomfortable. She tested herself by writing a letter declining the offer, and as soon as the last line was complete, doubt set in. Her head was saying, stay. Her gut was gnawing at her to go for the new and different challenge.

On the phone one Sunday morning, I urged her to be true to herself: 'Trust your gut Susan'. On Monday she did, and within a year she was chief executive with a mandate from the Minister to merge two smaller agencies into hers. Susan's inner voice had been right.

Gut feeling works
Both experts and lay people who rely on gut feeling make good decisions almost all of the time.

A gut feeling or hunch is a judgement that is made quickly, the underlying reasons for which we are not fully aware, and which is sufficiently strong to be acted on. Gut decisions are based on simple rules of thumb and the evolved capacity of our brains. Gerd Gigerenzer explains 'evolved capacity' as the subconscious ability to recognize patterns of information. The medical specialist with years of experience who spends just a few minutes with a patient and reaches a diagnosis that, after further examination, numerous laboratory tests, and a second opinion, is shown to be correct, is a classic example of pattern recognition.

Research evidence shows that in the final stages of a decision gut is right more often than detailed analysis and logic. One of the important reasons for this finding is that gut feelings ignore a great deal of the available information. The brain subconsciously screens out most of the surrounding data, searches for a pattern it recognizes, applies the resulting rule of thumb, and a decision emerges as a gut feeling. If you want to learn more about the science that informs this conclusion I commend Gerd Gigerenzer's book, especially chapter 3, to you. After reading his pithy, provocative little book, I hope like me you will be even more confident that you can take short cuts in making better decisions.

How often have you said this?
"I wish I had listened to my inner voice". We all have said this in one way or another many times in our lives. Not listening to what your body is telling you deprives you of vital information, more often than not just prior to making a decision. Hours, days, even weeks later with regret you say to yourself "I wish I had trusted my intuition".

Logic and reasoning all too often drown out your inner voice. Your rational tendency to gather and analyze facts and listen to others consumes your attention. And you, like all of us, are at risk of confirmation bias, paying attention to only those facts that point to what you think you want.

Being aware – in the moment – of how you are feeling is a skill that can be learned and improved with conscious practice. Stop, ask yourself 'How am I feeling right now? What is my body telling me?' As a leader in dealing with others, especially when there is stress or pressure to make a decision, stopping to listen to yourself is, often *the best,* way to make come to a conclusion. In the final moments when all options are analyzed and on the table, follow your instinct. You won't regret it. The probability of your judgement being flawed is slim.

Analysis and logic do have a place, but not on their own

With a doctorate in marketing science I need no persuading of the power and value of analysis and logic. But as a practicing psychologist who works with executives every day and as an observer of myself, I also know that listening to my inner voice has stood me in good stead when difficult trade-offs have to be made.

In other words, our gut feelings are a complement to logic and reasoning, and more often than not the final arbiter in making good decisions.

In conclusion

Warren Bennis wrote: *"A part of whole-brain thinking includes learning to trust what's been...called the 'blessed impulse', the hunch, the vision that shows you in a flash the absolutely right thing to do. Everyone has these visions; leaders learn to trust them."*

Related posts

You may want to delve into other aspects of this topic:

+ Manage your emotions better: Replace your musts and shoulds with wants and wishes http://www.beatonexecutivecoaching.com/manage-emotions-better-replace-musts-shoulds-wants-wishes/

+ How you can make better choices about your life and career http://www.beatonexecutivecoaching.com/how-you-can-make-better-choices-about-your-life-and-career/

………..

The original article can be found at http://www.beatonexecutivecoaching.com/trust-gut-make-better-decisions/. It is reprinted with permission from Dr. Margaret Beaton.

Appendix C

This appendix provides a news article noting some of the decision making differences between the US Army and the German Army.

Staff Group Explores German Decision Process

By Lt. Col. Hagen Ruppelt, German Army
Special to the Fort Leavenworth Lamp

Photo by Prudence Siebert, Fort Leavenworth Lamp

Caption: *German Lt. Col. (General Staff) Hagen Ruppelt and Marine Maj. Chuck Anklam listen to Air Force Maj. John Scott's briefing as they and their*

Command and General Staff Officer Course Staff Group 3A classmates transition from applying the German military decision-making process the week before to the U.S. military decision-making process in the Gray Horse-Raider Exercise, a pilot to see if the U.S.-British Eagle Owl exercise model could be expanded using the U.S.-German model, March 7 at the Lewis and Clark Center.

Staff Group Explores German Decision Process

Over the last two weeks, you may have seen an unusual increase in foreign uniforms on post. As in previous years, delegations of British and German field-grade officers have been attending the Eagle Owl planning exercise at the Command and General Staff College from Feb. 29 to March 10. Eagle Owl has become an inherent part of the brigade operations curriculum for all students of the Command and General Staff Officer Course.

This year, the exercise was unique for the students of Staff Group 3A. For the first time in the history of CGSC, they executed the German Army decision-making process and proved the success of that pilot project.

Together with their integrated international officers from Yemen and Germany, Staff Group 3A was augmented by one German staff officer, Maj. Stefan Kuhles from the Führungsakademie in Hamburg, Germany. With this new German flavor, different from all other staff groups, which had a British or U.S. focus, an exercise rename was warranted. Based on the heraldic animal of the German Panzerbrigade 21 and the motto of the American 1/4 Stryker Brigade Combat Team, Staff Group 3A named the operation "Gray Horse-Raider." Executing the German Army decision-making process, the U.S. students of Staff Group 3A experienced a new perspective on problem solving. This approach fostered teamwork within the multinational exercise staff, serving as a model for future American-German cooperation.

As the resident German student assigned to Staff Group 3A, I introduced the basic procedures and philosophy of the German planning process to my classmates the week before the exercise. The U.S. students learned that mission command, creative and innovative thinking, a strong role for the chief of staff and a consistent focus on conclusions are the main characteristics of the German problem-solving approach. Serving as the chief of staff, I guided my classmates through the new process for a stability operation on the African continent.

"It is a different approach that allows me to think critically," said U.S. Army Maj. Joe Didomenico, one of the U.S. students of Staff Group 3A.

U.S. Army Maj. Brian Weightman, who was assigned as the S2 for the exercise, was very enthusiastic, saying, "We will be able to put a lot of different planning tools in their kitbags for future assignments."

Throughout the exercise, the staff group prepared and briefed both U.S. and German officers, including U.S. Army Col. John Allred, director of CGSC's Department of Army Tactics; German Army Col. Ralf Broszinski, director of the German Führungsakademie Army Tactics Department; German Army Col. Carsten Treder, German liaison officer to the Combined Arms Center; German Army Lt. Col. Michael von Block Schlesier, head of the German exchange delegation; and German Army Lt. Col. Michael Kopp, the German exchange instructor in the CGSC Department of Army Tactics.

During the exercise, students had to transition from conceptual to detailed planning and build a comprehensive understanding of a complex and ill-structured operational environment. Considering the legal implications, social network analysis, and multi-national capabilities was a significant challenge in the scenario.

Despite the difficult setting, U.S. Army Maj. Daria Toler explained, "When comparing the U.S. and the German process, I saw more similarities than differences."

U.S. Army Maj. Neil Stark had the impression that the German process provided, "...more latitude to the chief of staff and flexibility for the staff to find innovative courses of action."

Other students took away that the German process that incorporates multiple staff synchronization meetings stimulates the necessary cross-section information exchange.

After the exercise, German Army Maj. Stefan Kuhles, the German reinforcement to Staff Group 3 A, was surprised saying, "I learned a lot about my own process during this week because we had very valuable dialogues within the staff about the development of recommendations that facilitate the decision-making for the commander."

Another important aspect of exercise Gray Horse-Raider was the teamwork that took place for the students.

The S4 and sustainment section leader, U.S. Army Maj. Peter Powell, explained, "All of us learned to collaboratively apply the new process and, more importantly, that we can trust each other."

In the end, Staff Group 3A and the assisting faculty were convinced that this new approach fostered mutual understanding among German and American students. This type of exchange activity facilitates problem-solving, outgoing and adaptive field grade officers for challenges in multinational operations. Overall, the exercise served as a promising pilot and has the potential to increase future cooperation between the U.S. Army Command and General Staff College and the Führungsakademie der Bundeswehr.

Published with permission from the Fort Leavenworth Lamp and LTC Ruppelt.
http://www.ftleavenworthlamp.com/article/20160310/NEWS/160309309/?tag=1

VII. References

Beaton, M. (2015) *Trust Your Gut and Make Better Decisions*, Retrieved from http://www.beatonexecutivecoaching.com/trust-gut-make-better-decisions May 19th 2016.

De Bono, E. (1985). *Six Thinking Hats* (1st U.S. ed.). Boston: Little, Brown.

Hammond, John S., Keeney, Ralph L., Raiffa, Howard (1998) *Even Swaps: A Rational Method for Making Trade-offs,* published in Harvard Business Review March 1998. Retrieved from https://hbr.org/1998/03/even-swaps-a-rational-method-for-making-trade-offs

Powell, C. (Date uncertain) *A Leadership Primer*, Retrieved from http://www.think-energy.net/Colin-Powell-on-Leadership.pdf March 2016

Raiffa, Howard, Hammond, John S., Keeney, Ralph L. (2006) *The Hidden Traps in Decision Making* published in Harvard Business Review January 2006.

Ruppelt, H. (2016) Staff Group Explorews German Decision Process, retrieved from http://www.ftleavenworthlamp.com/article/20160310/ NEWS/160309309/?tag=2_ 1 December 2016

Russo, J. and Shoemaker, P. (2002). *Winning Decisions*. New York: Currency Book, Random House.

Surowiecki, J. (2005). *The Wisdom of Crowds*. New York: Anchor Books.

Van Vliet, J. (2012). *Business and Public Policy*. Young Harris College text, ISBN 978-1478295211, CreateSpace, Young Harris, Georgia

Welch, J. (2013) *When To Go With Your Gut*, Retrieved from https://www.linkedin.com/pulse/20131112125301-86541065-when-to-go-with-your-gut February 2016

Notes

Notes

Made in the USA
Columbia, SC
31 October 2022

70265820R00055